THE MOUTH OF WHICH YOU ARE

poems by

Jenna Lynch

Finishing Line Press
Georgetown, Kentucky

THE MOUTH OF WHICH YOU ARE

For Adam

Copyright © 2018 by Jenna Lynch
ISBN 978-1-63534-771-5 First Edition
All rights reserved under International and Pan-American Copyright Conventions. No part of this book may be reproduced in any manner whatsoever without written permission from the publisher, except in the case of brief quotations embodied in critical articles and reviews.

ACKNOWLEDGMENTS

Many thanks to the editors of these publications in which the following poems, or versions of them, originally appeared:

Stirring: "Ideas About Mothers"
Sundog Lit: "Caul"
Construction Magazine: "In Transit" and "A Saturday Night"
Potluck Mag: "The Mouth of Which You Are" and "Emma Eckstein"
Forklift, Ohio: "Sonnet after Alice Notley"
Newtown Literary: "Something Rejected"

Publisher: Leah Maines
Editor: Christen Kincaid
Cover Art and Design: Rob Pizzolato
Author Photo: Valerie Senior

Printed in the USA on acid-free paper.
Order online: www.finishinglinepress.com
also available on amazon.com

Author inquiries and mail orders:
Finishing Line Press
P. O. Box 1626
Georgetown, Kentucky 40324
U. S. A.

Table of Contents

Caul 1

The Mouth of Which You Are 2

Something Rejected 3

With Your Eyes Alone..4

Ahriman & Ormuzd 6

Sonnet after Alice Notley..8

Inthewrongplaceness..9

A Young Freud, on a Long Train Journey, Remembers his
   Mother Undressing 10

A Letter from Freud October, 1896.............................12

Emma Eckstein 13

A Saturday Night 14

Summering at Norman Mailer's House 15

In Transit 16

Trigger Warning 17

After Ted Berrigan..18

Gone 19

Ideas about Mothers...20

Weekends..21

Washington Square Park in Noon Light....................22

Those Last Days 23

To My Lost Naomi...24

The Kayak Killer 25

Window, Water, Baby, Moving...................................27

Mothlight..28

Memories of Charlotte Delbo 29

Notes 33

CAUL

I was born in mine—
looped around the ears like her fingers,
the *wish-phantasy of flight from the world,*

ballooned from between her swollen legs—
I must have looked faceless, or maybe
like the Imboden photograph, *Sainthood,*
my face rising from the split of her body as if
from water.

The midwife unhooked my veil,
peeled it back, and gave it to my mother,
who, years later,
ground it to a powder,
fed it to me with the white
of an egg.

Now, my fear is not of water,
or drowning—
or being entered by someone both unnamed
and unfathered, but instead
of the re-birth, the return to the womb,
a bell-flower membrane masking
my head.

THE MOUTH OF WHICH YOU ARE

You don't think of those around you when you utter mommy
under your breath: *I love her, I eat her, I bite her,*
something enters your mouth, your mouth as womb,

asshole, ear. The woman whose daughter is dead speaks loudly
to you about loss, about forgetting—realizing the difference between
"being away" and "being dead," how you have to be dead to never
 come back,
how she likes that part, remembers Freud's four-year-old in the
 footnote:
but why won't father be home for supper?

Later, in a different city, to a room full of strangers, you insist
that your mouth is your best idea on the basis of agreement, silence,
even and deliberate tone, on the entrance of language that is separate,
 unrecorded.

You are suddenly aware of distance. Kristeva says, the mother inhabits
 the mouth,
the lungs, the digestive tube of her baby: accompanying her echolalia,
leading the way to stories and sentences: *a speaking subject.*
The body doubled up and made *sacred.*

Remember you used to say *ma ma ma,* three steps down the palate,
 tap tap tap.
Remember your wish for a mirror that won't reflect the face of your
 mother,
for two mouths, mother tongue—for a mouth in another room, in a
 different body.

SOMETHING REJECTED

As in Joon-ho's *Mother*, you must loosen the ties,
return to a state of isolation: not
Eros, which absorbs or rejects but does not sever,
but rather *Thanatos*: death-bearing—

the inside mixed with the unstable border
of the mother's body.

Bellini, having been loved by no mother,
painted Madonnas for a lifetime. Madonna
the Mother *dreaming of an unsignifiable experience.*
Mother with the Child *parallel and close,*
the clean and proper body,
that mute border.

One kind of son asks his mother to wash
his hair in the kitchen sink. Another drinks
from the bowl in her hand as he pisses against the wall.

There are things you have to say
that you can write down in your notebook for now,
little fits of dread, *a vomiting of the mother.*

She presses the bowl to Do-joon's lips,
but different this time, not laced with poison.
She says, *you and I are one*, her devouring body,
his piss and shit and blood,

your leaking borders,
Bellini's movement towards color and light—
that luminous *outside.*

WITH YOUR EYES ALONE

You lick the tip of a cigarette, push the tobacco against the sting,
hold it against your head while he looks for a poem.

Reception for first year graduate students,

everyone pretending to be interested,
pretending to hear what the other is saying, holding

tightly to plastic cups as they circle the room. He's ready to leave,
but you want to stick around a while,

inhabit another self for an hour or two,
your mouth a gaping hole of hysterics, and hands that hurt.

Lately everyone is giving you advice to "take it easy"
when you could be coming from behind,

your hair pulled back, his pierced cock with prince's wand, neck bites,
memories of those mornings of early consciousness—

Ginsberg's key in the window, letters from his mother urging
        marriage, clean living,

              her wishing strongly he was someone else,

her with *the long black beard around the vagina.*

Instead you want to know everything, even what doesn't matter:

oxblood colored trousers, black spike heel booties, removable collars
in the copy of Vogue, Fall issue, the one with Keira Knightley on the
  cover,

hair piece that makes a kind of shield—

        all things worth knowing,

like his hands now, thumb and index making a steeple on his chin.

The girl behind you asks,   "can I have a sip of water," then,
"aren't you listening?"

But you're thinking of something else, you forget to answer, close your
  eyes
for a second to catch your breath.

And you know now things will never be easy:
you look in a mirror and see   mother, brother, twin, shadow, skeleton—

you are anything you want,

        even a little boy.

You light the cigarette backwards, with a hand shading your face,

with a face like hers,

with his face open, talking.

AHRIMAN & ORMUZD

I imagine a type of violent splitting: 2 boys
tearing from the womb: Ahriman, *the Angry Spirit*,
fighting to be the first, dropping his brother's hand
he emerges wet and bloody from his father, from
Zurva, his body uncurling—
only to find a room full of light,
everything untouched, virginal.

—but it isn't like that; there was no birth,
no light-filled room, this is all metaphor,
a story told at childhood:
it is Zarathustra on the bridge calling upon
us all to choose,

but we're left standing, not ready yet,
alone with the hovering feeling, something like
a ghost-limb, a search for the other
half of a knucklebone, *symbolon*:

but what if I want the *druj*, the evil, the spirit of the lie,
what if I want it too.

Cadere, to fall.
When made to look at a corpse
for the first time, I came face to face
with my repulsion: I gave birth
to my own body, or my body—it fell
beyond limit—cadaver, *I fall in a faint.*

I imagine I am standing
at the bridge of the petitioner, the dead
souls rising all around me, taking shape
again, and I want to lie down and listen but
the ground is cold under my shoes—

and it's my self divided: the one me
toeing the line, teetering
on the edge of the final renovation—
the other perched above, or
slung over my shoulder, urging me to *go*,

quick, jump.

SONNET AFTER ALICE NOTLEY

"You must" "be willing to" "try anything,"
"even" "what scares you." "Like all" "that occurs"
"in secret:" "mugwort tucked" "in shoes," "a string
tied to" "2 chicken bones," "all things" "absurd,"

"ritual over." "How" "desire can conflict"
"with morality;" "the edges of" "eyelids," "of tongues;"
"our love is" "an edge" "(O love!)" "our teeth, picked"
"clean, bright" "white," "like sage," "bundles passed over lungs:"

"all" "things healing," "like" "my mouth," "inviting
spirits:" "swallowing," "deep yawning." "The border
between" "I" "and" "Other" "as" "*most fragile,*" "biting
as" "threat: a red mouth" "devouring a daughter,"

"the mouth I fill" "with words," "the words I use" "on you"
"like raspberry syrup:" "sweet," "an edge to cut" "through."

INTHEWRONGPLACENESS
After Kira O'Reilly's performance piece of the same title

Whose skin is whose? At first it's hard to tell, her hand pressed
firmly against the pig's back, propping him up. The sign on the
door reads: *don't do anything you don't want to.*

The window with the view of Market Jew Street and statue of
   Humphry Davy
does little to contain the contents of this space:

naked woman body, freshly slaughtered pig; small hand-mirror
   to reflect death infecting life.

I am alone in the room with them, almost an intrusion, my hands
   gloved in latex with the promise "to touch both animal and
   human flesh."

Kira O'Reilly has rehearsed this scene four times. The pig as
   dummy, stand-in, twin, doll.
As *Other Self.* Those piggy bits: a substitute, a stunt double.

Her hair is wet, with what?—sweat, blood? A slow drag of flesh
   across the carpet,
she is nourishing the corpse, the border becoming object:

both confrontation and collapse, then start again.

She puts her entire head into the chest cavity of the pig; the
   inside of the pig.
Next to them: taxidermied piglet with the missing leg.

This final scene: a merging of selves. One living, one dead.

My gloved and sterile hand moves over their bodies in one
   motion. Confusing human and nonhuman, I caress, touch, feel,
   stroke. A flickering of The Body,

a collapsing of boundaries,

that pink pig flesh so much like my own.

A YOUNG FREUD, ON A LONG TRAIN JOURNEY, REMEMBERS HIS MOTHER UNDRESSING

Sitting snug in this train car, Leipzig to Vienna,
pondering Goethe's skull on the Lido,
hoping for enlightenment, I picture a bath in reddish

water, a chain of memories, the awakening
of my libido towards *matrem*: water in which
she had previously washed herself. I see her, *nudam*:

the woman-mother's naked, whole body,
lipsticked and stockinged, the sharpness of her shoulder
blades, the soft curve of her belly in the frame

of the hotel window: the architecture of those lines
as smooth and familiar as my own hands
in front me now, touching the tops of my thighs,

holding firm to a pen as I write my dearest Lou.
Strange now, to have no feeling of shame, for which
there should well be occasion.
I close my eyes, press them
shut against this memory of my mother.

And what makes me think of her now,
with her one foot propped on the sill, bending

to undo the buckle of her heel, sweat
brightening the hollow around
her collarbone.

I want to say something now about the look
of your body against my reflection in the glass,
slim and beautiful, about my hands
reaching out, cupped as in offering to you.

Say I was there. Say I am here now, *sitting alone
in my wagon-lit compartment,*
as I talk to myself to let the details go,
letting the light out.

A LETTER FROM FREUD
October, 1896

Dearest Father,

In my dream, your body is uncoffined
before me, a sign above reads:

"Close the eyes."

And I want to listen. To keep them shut.
But every time I wake to another
dead father.

I uncovered your gift today, removed
it from a drawer: a newly bound
Bible, a letter pressed dry between its pages.
It's been since my 35th that I've read:

*Behold it! I present this as an offering,
from your father who loves you.*

And do your thoughts dwell
upon me still? You, whose
body is on display,
your one greatest request.

And if only we could define son
without death.

I'm so filled with absence
even the railway cars don't mean
the same, another
sleeping body in a wagon-lit compartment.

In your memory I leave you
with this letter, this paper I press
against my face, that I seal
with a spot of blood.

Your,
Sigm.

EMMA ECKSTEIN

The room is a flush of white light,
a continuous hum of those
parasitic plants that invade my life.

He speaks to me as one might speak
to his drugged mother, slowly, carefully
so as not to confuse, *keep very still.*

They thumb shut my eyelids, a swab of cocaine
for the pain, scorpion's kiss,
memory dissolving into bedsheets,
the purulent secretion draining into my pillow.

Can the friend that stabs you—
the steel scalpel pulled slowly across flesh,
a bone chip the size of a Heller dropped
into a clean silver bowl—be the love that

they pull and pull on, the thread?
Afterwards: a half meter of gauze,
my blood a flood of red on my face
and neck.

I lie back, nose swaddled in bandages,
eyes bulged out like plums,
my face bloated and ugly, a sticky clot
filmed on my lips, marrowy flakes stuck
to my chin.

Tomorrow, I will look in the mirror
and not recognize
my face, the nose I once admired
chiseled away, caved in.

My hand reaches between
my legs. Watch what dreams I see.

Peel off the bandages
and have a look at me.

A SATURDAY NIGHT
For Thom Gunn

Met him at The Boiler Room
In the Village, he was
Wearing Fred Perry, jeans tight,
Cool smile. He rolled his tongue around
The neck of a beer and I fell
In love. Maybe
He's a skinhead, or

Maybe I just don't care,
As long as he puts his
Mouth on me. What I'm searching
For is contact: full-bodied lust,
The walk without the shame. My whole
Entire face
Is pressed up against

The bathroom stall. His breath
Is hot in my ear; teeth
Tracing my jaw line. Pushed
Into my hand, soft flesh turning hard:
Before long: his mouth an O shape
Around my cock,
My mouth sucked-in, feet

Jammed forward against tile.
I remember I want
To be him, to be him in-
Side me: have I been here before?
I was hot for experience,
Hot for impulse.
My body I could

Own, his body I could
Occupy. His torso
Lean like my father's. Something
I recognize, like a fist inside
My flesh, knuckled, kneading, scraping:
Where do we come
Apart in sex?

SUMMERING AT NORMAN MAILER'S HOUSE
Provincetown, Massachusetts

She leads me up the back stairs,
gives me a tour of the place,
the library overlooking the stilled water,
the master bedroom with the antique vanity
and mustard-green carpet,

turning every gold knob carefully, her hands,
the same ones that search for mine
in the dark of the hallway, nails much longer
than my own.

Looking up at her, I know
I am the first—her eyes wide like someone
surprised at her own reflection in a mirror.

We leave all the lights on and
the windows open to the sounds of bikes
cruising down Commercial Street, bears riding
in packs to get to the bar.

And I wonder what else began and ended in this room:
room of orgies, room of sitting still, room of come
any closer and I'll shoot.

Norris, did you hang this floral paper? Or was it one of the five
women before you who decided the warmth of this space?

It's not hard to fool the one who loves you.

The window's breeze raises the hairs
on her arms and I'm reminded of the salted air,
Kunitz's garden, men in drag
celebrating freedom.

She rolls over to face me,

opens her mouth like someone talking while sneezing—
like another woman's face altering as I enter.

IN TRANSIT

I'm writing you from the back of the Greyhound. We pass
Yonkers, Woodlawn, Riverdale,
people doing nothing in the street,
a body asleep on the sidewalk, or passed
out, it doesn't matter—what I mean to say is,
how are you?

It's quiet here, in the back of the bus,
my face pressed up against the greasy glass,
the woman next to me is resting lightly
on my shoulder—but outside the city screams:

And I think of us, reeling down St. Mark's Place,
freshly tattooed and sweaty,
bleeding black ink through my jeans,
you, a heart burning a hole in my chest.

And somewhere someone's writing
dyke across a telephone booth,
a brick wall, the hood of a car—
but we're here, kissing in the greasy
streets of Manhattan, flipping off cars
and old men who flick their tongues
in our direction, hoping for a taste.

In response to your question:
I don't love you, at least not in a way
you understand (What is there
if not honesty, a good ear, a place to
call home?) Here, in a cab
cutting across 5th avenue,
on the 6 train to Grand Central,
and every time it ends.

                                        This view is
anything but regular—
cool and flat: my hand
on your chest.

TRIGGER WARNING

In the movie, the father, mistaking his son
for someone else,
doesn't recognize his small frame in the dark
shadows of the barn, sends a bullet
through his thigh.

He lays his body down in the still-wet grass.

They say a corpse that lies down
can cast no shadow; the departed ghost:
like breath through the nostrils,
that little white cloud—

in the darkness, like in sleep,
the soul left his body

the way we leave others,
a quick movement of vapor,

a scent that lingers long after you've gone.

AFTER TED BERRIGAN

                              "Dear T_____,

It's 1:03 a.m. in Provincetown, early July heat, yes,
it's the week of the bear. The men spill into the streets
in packs yellow and brown, hair gleaming
under winking moon. I'm peeling the skin off my mouth,
I'm enclosing it in this letter, quick cut of lightning across
the sky as I write this, man and woman next door
grilling tortillas on an open flame, standing all agog
on the patio, whistling, talking. This morning,
I woke early, wandered around the house,
watched the sun come up over the water so I could write
it down in my notebook, drank coffee, ran errands,
thought about this letter, of you.
It's 1:21 a.m., I am licking the stamp, the sweet lugubrious glue
staining my tongue, melting in the steady heat of this night.
                                        As ever, yours."

GONE

The crowded street, a watery moon
against thick August heat, a little drunk
you said, *How long I've wanted
my mouth on you.* Remember?

How I used to tell you my dreams,
how in them you're holding me up,
I can barely stand.

Now, days pass between us like breath,
the sun sinking slowly into fog, a bending
of pale light through clouds, waking up
searching for your body. For months now,
I've lived with absence— a hovering
like the dead.

You're still here, though
I never much see you anymore.
I can taste the heat from chili peppers
that once made us undress, your upper lip
salted with sweat—
I can taste that too.

A cradling: walking past Clarke's
Funeral Chapel, rain heavy around me,
the melting sun pooling yellow
in the cheekbones of every passerby—

I think of you, of O'Hara's heart
closing like a fist, of a poem I dreamed
that ends: *this emptiness
I carry around like guilt.*

IDEAS ABOUT MOTHERS

It has nothing to do with you and you're walking around with the idea of mothers again, like Brakhage, lowering himself onto his naked wife's body in Wedlock House, her nipples glowing, his lips not quite sure where to go. He lights her cigarette, the scene flashes to the windowpane, the alarm clock reads midnight, or noon. Maybe he is remembering his mother, or not-remembering the woman who abandoned him at birth, how she looked up without crying, looked right into his face. How the voice probably never said *What have I done?* How there was no turning back and she never did anyway. Mother. Mommy. Wife. Woman. Bitch. Or as mother: scum, mold, the sediment of wine, the filmy layer in fermenting liquors that shows itself, rising to the surface. As an adult, Freud visited his mother every Sunday, he brought her flowers, he thought about her naked, scar on his chin that reminds him of her—how long until you realize you are no longer dreaming? A woman, driving her children into a lake, can't get her story straight, forgets to factor in the traffic lights, the empty streets, the timing of green to red, the permanency of green. She also forgets to drive quickly, rolls the car into the water, watches it drift. Decades later and she's lying on her back somewhere, maybe wishing she used the tub, or a baby pool, I guess they weren't old enough to wash themselves, she'd say. There are worse ways to go, she'd say. You are talking to your mother on the phone and you forget where home is, you have no memory. Her voice is so high.

WEEKENDS

Weekends are long and unfeeling,
wet dreams of the night congealing
on the bedsheets. She is in the other room
cleaning out her glass, working a mushroom
that has dried against the sink.
What would her mother think—
I have a confession, she turns
the words over in her mind, burns
her fingers on the faucet. Things change.
It is no great secret. Daughters exchange
mothers for other lovers, for things that break,
the curve of her back, a familiar handshake.
The weekends turning slowly over,
a hand on the cheek that does not waiver.

WASHINGTON SQUARE PARK IN NOON LIGHT

Stretched flat on his back,
hat over his face, arms spread out
on either side, the man is unmoving,

nothing under him, palms up and open
as if asking forgiveness, or waiting for change
to be dropped from heaven, or someone's pocket.

For a moment I imagine him not breathing,
his heart failing, no one noticing, or thinking
to notice, stepping over him in a hurry,
nudging him accidentally with a sneaker,
a dog sniffing his crotch.

I imagine lifting the cap off and seeing a dead
stare, eyes fixed on the sky, glassed,
his mouth open in an unanswered prayer,
or around a lover's name.

I imagine I am the lover, maybe sleeping gently
on his shoulder, or maybe bathing
and drying his tired feet.

Minutes go by, watching, the sunlight hitting
his covered face, his arms motionless,
pinned to the earth as on an invisible cross.

THOSE LAST DAYS

his body fragile like a child's,
my mother cradled him in her arms
like she did me once, his paws
hanging over her soft forearm:

> *He has never left me, loved me unconditionally,
> slept with me in bed when I was sick for days.*

She insisted we call the vet.
He couldn't stand anymore,
or walk on his own—
she carried him everywhere:
to eat or sleep or piss.

Coming home from work,
my mother found a pile of him,
immovable: *I know what I have to do,*

but he passed before she could
make the appointment, my father
waking to find the two of them
together in bed: the dog
not breathing, lying stiff
on my mother's pillow,
just above her head.

Cosmo, you loved her better
than I ever could. You loved her
without knowing any other way.

Now she sits alone again, without you,
no one to cook for or talk to, the blued
glow of the television keeping her warm,
your collar tucked away in the nightstand.

TO MY LOST NAOMI
After Allen Ginsberg

Mother—to think of you now
with your too-thin wrists, streak of gray
      across the hairline, complaining
of vertigo—and your ragged scars from
the caesarian, and the bruised bags that hang
under your eyes that you keep open each night studying me, searching
      for my name, for clues

And I think of how we all suffer,
and you too
 -your loneliness, your boredom
      your missing teeth—those empty sockets

you with pinched cheeks and
sundried lips

I see you still—staying up late, measuring the length of my nails,
      your mind accelerating towards thoughts of repentance

and your shame, it spread—
was the entire floor for a moment, it seemed—
what were you thinking then
         and did you ever want to be me?

      Mother, we've all moved on

the rumors around town, the ones I heard
   from friends, you crying in Church,
praying for me, trying to save me

close your eyes now, it's almost over
    I'll never be saved
        Mother

THE KAYAK KILLER

How does she do it—
remove the drain plug from his kayak—?

Discreetly, probably
              gingerly maybe,

    like I do
uncorking a day-old bottle
of red wine
        to drink in secret—

        something intentional,   like lying

like forgetting to pack the life jacket.

A reaction to a lover's violent attempts at seduction,
a complicated relationship with pornography

        because a man says
                I must surrender to the beast that I am

And what does she feel, then, as the
boat slowly fills with water?

Relief perhaps
                or freedom.

Her toe pushes his paddle away   gently
        as only a woman could.

When I read her plea of guilty
I almost smiled.

But not for the right reasons, no instead

    for the shared relief:

the shedding of something darker
than even yourself.

She kept the plug in the dash
of the car to remind her—

    I wanted him dead
                and now he's gone—

kept it as I keep this:

a woman without secrets
                will always be lost.

WINDOW, WATER, BABY, MOVING
After the film of the same title by Stan Brakhage

She lowers herself into the bath,
her belly swollen and heavy,
one hand on her back, the other
bracing the bathroom wall.
He slips his fingers beneath the water
to ease her pain, pushing the abdomen as she cries.
The swimmer inside her
makes its way to her surface,
splitting her slowly,
crowning, pushing, leaving
the sealed world.
She can't remember what she learned
to feel at this moment. She talks to herself:
this water's too hot,
what if he stops breathing.
Her reflection in the windowpane
looks too much like herself.
The afterbirth follows,
packed like raspberries, wet and shining.
She thinks then of the lotus birth,
blood and veins and tissue she has raised,
growing from her new life's center,
twinned, bound to him
until it becomes too much to carry,
until it dries and curls and then drops,
leaving him alone on the carpet, screaming.
His face is wet with the inside
of her body, skin blue, hanging
by the ankles delicately in the midwife's hands
until the life rushes down, red, pink, sudden.

MOTHLIGHT

> *"What a moth would probably see between birth and death, if black was white and white was black"* —Stan Brakhage

Together the moths fly, fluttering their wings,
bodies batting against each other, these things
not living but dead, remains on the film strip fed
through the projector, life given back instead.

Bodied projections flash against the sky,
flowering of layered shapes, movements to trick the eye.
In the light life is left, the moths press on the screen,
wings pinned to leaves, stuck to a constructed world of green.

The wings, pressed between layers of tape,
are dancing, streams of light giving shape
to what to them must feel like love—pools of brightness
they long for, flock to, even when bodies are bloodless.

MEMORIES OF CHARLOTTE DELBO

I. The Common and the Deep

Through a knothole in the wood of the car
you memorize the stops along the train line,

names, you each took turns reading them.

Singing to keep from freezing

> *(We're Frenchwomen!—*
> *let's march, let's march! That an impure brow*
> *waters our furrows)—*

Auschwitz:

it is there, encased in the skin
of your memory.

Nothing can pass through,
unalterable,

forever isolated, and forever

close—

The Auschwitz double: one
of you lives inside,
the other: next to it,

pressed up
against its skin—

The skin of Auschwitz
like the skin of the dead,

of Viva,

tight and transparent, holding her bones, cradling
her sternum, her cranium (*she used to have
beautiful shoulders, Viva*).

All around you
the bodies are piling up.

Naked,
                      (each body is a shout)

pubic hair, stiff and straight,
toes stuck up in the snow.

In heaps,
seen from the steady rise of soup steam
through the window.

Throughout roll call
you never look at the corpses:

Try to look. Just try and see.

II. Roll Call

They have us stand for hours,
a pattern forming
in the blackened snow:

from above,
we must look like marbles
lined in rows,
heads naked,

every inch
shaved and swabbed,
made sexless by hunger.

We are joined only
by the need
to keep standing.

The gypsy woman
clutches a bundle
of rags to her chest,

her baby's face
bluish and waxy from the cold—

It's dead, isn't it?

We wait.
We wait for day

because one must wait for something.

And those,
the ones that have not
made it through
cross past us on stretchers—

She lasted a long time, that one.

A whole winter. A whole spring.

III

They make our mothers strip right in front of us:
My mother as hands, torso, face.

They strip the dead bodies naked.
Their clothes will be worn by the others.
We are all destined for a naked death.
Our nakedness makes them happy.

If you look close enough at the bodies piled
in the snow, you can almost see them move,
fingers opening slowly,
tattoos to identify.

We are told to remove the bodies from the field,
the dead women left in the field.
One is still alive, hanging onto
my ankles, begging.

Yesterday, they were hungry.
Yesterday, they slurped down gruel.
Yesterday, they were exhausted and beaten.
Yesterday, they wished to die.

Now they are lying frozen.
Now their toes are cocked up in the snow.
Now they are dead on block 25
because they fainted at roll call,
were paler than the others.

Notes

In "Something Rejected," the line *dreaming of an unsignifiable experience* is quoted from Julia Kristeva's *Desire in Language: A Semiotic Approach to Literature and Art* (Columbia University Press, 1980).

In "Ahriman & Ormuzd," words and phrases in italics are quoted from Kristeva's *The Powers of Horror: An Essay on Abjection* (Columbia University Press, 1982).

In "A Young Freud, on a Long Train Journey, Remembers his Mother Undressing," words and phrases are borrowed from Sigmund Freud's letters to Wilhelm Fliess (1887-1904), Harvard University Press.

The titled speaker in "Memories of Charlotte Delbo" was a French writer who was sent to Auschwitz for her role as a member for the French resistance. The lines *We're Frenchwomen!—let's march, let's march! That an impure brow waters our furrows* are the translated lyrics to "La Marseillaise," the national anthem of France. All other italics in the poem are quoted from Delbo's book, *Auschwitz and After* (Yale University Press, 1985), a first-person account of her experiences in Birkenau.

I offer my grateful acknowledgement for the inspiration given to me from these writers' works.

Additional Acknowledgements

I am grateful to the Vermont Studio Center, for the generous fellowship and support that enabled me the time and space to complete this collection. It was there that I not only grew as a writer, but also met many lifelong friends.

To Garrett Hongo, for the constant encouragement, and for pushing me to think deeply and critically, and to trust my voice; this book would not be possible without your guidance.

To Elizabeth Arnold, for teaching me form, and laying the foundation for my poetic studies.

To Hannah Baker Saltmarsh and Lindsay Bernal, for serving as my undergraduate mentors—my enduring thanks for your thoughtful and honest feedback and first workshop experiences, and for giving me such strong female role models to look up to.

To Julia Kolchinsky Dasbach, for being a loyal reader and travelling with me into the darkness of many of these poems and helping me through them, as well as for your friendship and endless support. Thank you.

Thank you to my partner, Brendan, for always believing in me and my work, and for never letting me give up. To my colleagues, friends, and family, my deepest gratitude for your support, friendship and love.

Jenna Lynch holds a B.A. in English Literature from the University of Maryland and an M.F.A. in Poetry from the University of Oregon. Her work has appeared in *Construction Magazine, The Westchester Review, Newtown Literary, Forklift, Ohio,* among others. She was named a finalist for the 2013 Joy Harjo Poetry Prize by *Cutthroat: A Journal of the Arts,* and has received fellowships and residencies at the Vermont Studio Center and the Norman Mailer Writers Colony. Jenna lives in Astoria, Queens.

www.ingramcontent.com/pod-product-compliance
Lightning Source LLC
LaVergne TN
LVHW041604070426
835507LV00011B/1303